Scout was a playful puppy who loved to explore the world around him.

His best friend was Summer, a kind chicken hen who liked to observe before jumping in.

Even though they were very different, Scout and Summer made a great team.

Almost every afternoon, they met at the park to play on the playground.

Scout raced up the ladder and zoomed down the slide.

Summer clucked happily from below, cheering him on.

They laughed, talked, and shared stories about their day.

When they finished playing, Scout reached into his bag for his puppy treats.

His eyes grew wide.
"My treats are gone!" Scout said.

Scout looked around the playground, then glanced at Summer.

"Summer," Scout asked slowly, "did you take my treats?"

Summer stood tall and shook her head. "No, Scout. I didn't take them," she said honestly.

"I would never do that to a friend," Summer added. "But I will help you find them."

Good friends tell the truth, even when things are confusing.

Scout felt unsure for a moment, but then he remembered something important.

"Okay," Scout said.
"I trust you. Let's look together."

They searched under the slide and beside the swings.

Summer flapped her wings and pointed with her beak.
"What about over there?"

Near the park bench, Scout spotted his bag.

Inside were his puppy treats, safe and untouched..

Scout's ears drooped for a moment. "I forgot where I put them," he said.

Summer smiled warmly.
"That's how friendship works," she said.

"I'm sorry I doubted you," Scout told Summer.
"Thank you for telling the truth."

Scout shared his treats, and Summer shared a happy cluck.

They sat together, enjoying the sunny day.

Scout learned that honesty builds trust.

And Summer showed that helping a friend matters just as much.

Being friendly and truthful made their friendship even stronger.

Scout and Summer walked home side by side.

They knew they could always count on each other.

Because honesty and friendship always go hand in hand.
The End

Thank you for taking the time to enjoy this story about friendship, trust, and honesty. The idea and plot entirely came from my son Riley, who was interested in writing a book with me one day. I had not thought about how impactful his story, and characters that he named himself, were going to be to other children his age when they read his story. Books are powerful, and the time you spend with your children is so key in their development, that I want to encourage all parents to find the time to make an impact in their children's lives. You just never know what may come of it. Thank you Riley, for spending that afternoon with me and being my co-pilot. Love You.

Made in the USA
Coppell, TX
28 February 2026

When Scout the puppy heads to the park for a fun day of play, he never expects to face a big problem, his favorite puppy treats suddenly go missing!
With the help of his best friend, Summer the chicken hen, Scout learns that friendship is built on trust, kindness, and honesty. As the two search the playground together, Scout discovers that jumping to conclusions can hurt feelings, but telling the truth can make friendships even stronger.
Scout and Summer Tell the Truth is a heartwarming story that teaches children ages 5-8 the importance of being honest, respectful, and friendly, even when things don't go as planned.

Key Lessons and Skills
- *Teaching honesty and trust*
- *Encouraging empathy and teamwork*
- *Shared reading at home or in the classroom*

A gentle, uplifting story that reminds young readers that honesty and friendship always go hand in hand.